ORCHESTRATED ARRANGEMENTS

by Ric Ianonne

CD TRACK LIST

Each piece/track includes a repeat.

This CD was recorded with the student part on the right channel and the orchestrated arrangements on the left channel.
The student's part can be muted by turning the balance all the way to the left.

	Page # in Book	Track # (Practice tempo)	Track # (Performance tempo)
The Bird's Song	4	1	2
Fun in the Sun!	6	3	4
Monkey Music	8	5	6
The Butterfly Waltz	10	7	8
Cool Grooves	12	9	10
Indian Village	14	11	12
Daydreams	16	13	14
Ghost Story	18	15	16
A Magic Carpet Ride	20	17	18
Crazy Clowns!	22	19	20

The enclosed audio CD is playable on any CD player.
For Windows® and Mac computer users, the CD is enhanced so you can access MIDI files for each song.

• This product is compatible with Windows 2000 and Windows XP using Internet Explorer.
• This product is compatible with Mac OS X using Safari.
(Enhanced features may not be available for Mac OS 9 and earlier.)

For technical support, please email **support@halleonard.com**.

BEANSTALK'S BASICS FOR
PIANO

PERFORMANCE BOOK
PREPARATORY
LEVEL

BY CHERYL FINN & EAMONN MORRIS

WILLIS MUSIC

12545

CONTENTS

A NOTE TO PARENTS AND TEACHERS

Beanstalk's Basics for Piano Performance Preparatory Level is written to encourage the young piano student to perform effectively from the earliest level. The level of these performance pieces corresponds directly with the materials covered in the **Beanstalk's Basics for Piano Preparatory A & B Lesson Books.** Each piece is marked with an **ENCORE!** box. Upon successfully playing the selection by memory, the student is rewarded with the matching colored sticker from the enclosed sticker sheet. The sticker is placed on the page to complete the illustration accompanying the piece.

Further, for successful performance of the piece by memory in a recital situation or in front of the teacher or parent, the student receives a performance sticker which is placed on the final page of the book.

We recommend that the teacher detach and retain the sticker sheet as the student begins each book. This preserves the element of surprise and increases motivation. Further, it ensures better control of the sticker allocation. Consideration of the **ENCORE!** box and the sticker reward for each piece is ideally withheld until the student is first able to perform the selection with all the appropriate musical elements in place.

May these be the first of many encore performances!

CHERYL FINN   EAMONN MORRIS

PERFORMANCE

HISTORY

The history of solo piano performance, like all history, is a fascinating and engaging story. Like all history, it too develops in stages. Did you know that up until the 19th century, keyboard musicians usually performed with written music in front of them? In fact, it is the very famous pianist and performer Clara Schumann (1819-1856) - wife of the composer Robert Schumann (1810-1856) - who is believed to have changed all that by first performing long and complex works by memory! Today most performers play from memory when giving concerts and recitals.

The solo piano concert is also a fairly recent development. While performers like Mozart (1756-1791) and Beethoven (1770-1827) played in royal courts and Chopin (1810-1849) played in the salons and drawing rooms of Paris, it wasn't until Franz Liszt (1811-1886) that the solo piano moved out into the larger concert hall. Liszt had enormous hands and his music is very rich and full, meaning that he had no trouble filling any hall with sound. Liszt was like a pop superstar in his time, with people lining up to buy tickets for his concerts and women in particular fainting at the sight of him playing.

PERFORMANCE TIPS

Here are some helpful hints for success in performance.

1. Bow gracefully. A bow is an important show of respect for the audience. Some performers bow after playing and some bow before and after. The choice of when to bow is something you may want to discuss with your teacher.

2. Make sure your bench is properly adjusted. Check that the bench is at a comfortable distance from the piano, not too close and not too far away. The audience will always have patience while you adjust or move the bench because they know this will help your performance.

3. After sitting down, wait a few seconds before you begin playing. That way you have some time to focus yourself on the job at hand. This time also makes you appear to be relaxed and unhurried. If you look relaxed the audience will relax and will enjoy your performance more!

4. Most of all, have fun! Remember that the people in your audience are there to support you and enjoy your playing. If you have fun they will too!

THE BIRD'S SONG

CORRESPONDS WITH PAGES 18 THROUGH 26 OF BEANSTALK'S LESSON BOOK PREP A.

12545

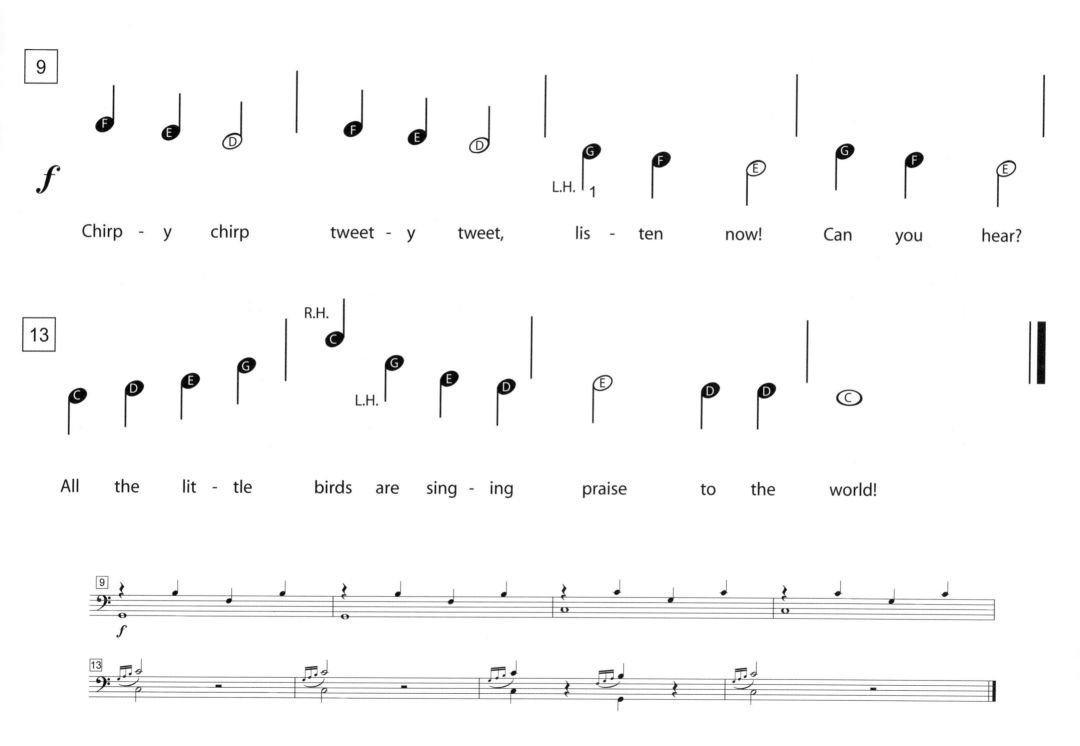

FUN IN THE SUN!

Happily

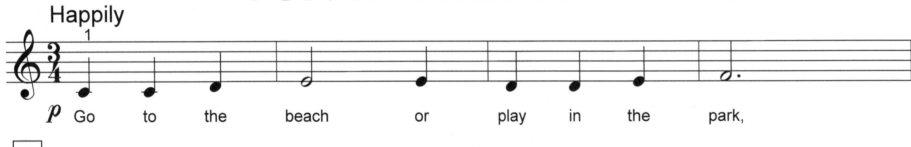

p Go to the beach or play in the park,

f off to a pic - nic, home be - fore dark.

Student plays one octave
higher than written.

Happily

Teacher
Duet
Part

CORRESPONDS WITH PAGES 28 THROUGH 35 OF BEANSTALK'S LESSON BOOK PREP A.

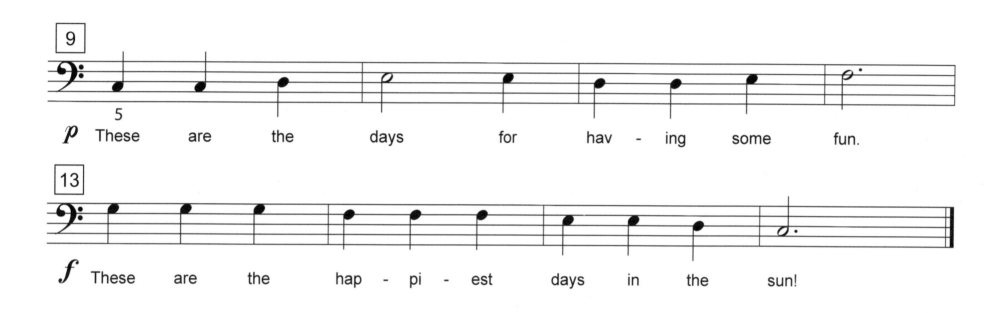

9

𝆏 These are the days for hav - ing some fun.

13

𝆑 These are the hap - pi - est days in the sun!

9

𝆏

13

𝆑

Happily

MONKEY MUSIC

ENCORE!

3. Memorized.

Mon - key   mu - sic is   funk - y,   too.

Mon - key   mu - sic for   me and   you!

Student plays one octave
higher than written.
Happily

Teacher
Duet
Part

8

CORRESPONDS WITH PAGES 37 THROUGH 42 OF BEANSTALK'S LESSON BOOK PREP A.

12545

THE BUTTERFLY WALTZ

Gracefully

Waltz - ing a - round on the scent of a sum - mer breeze,

Car - ried a - round on a wing and a song.

Student plays two octaves higher than written.

Gracefully

Teacher Duet Part

con pedale

10

CORRESPONDS WITH PAGES 43 THROUGH 47 OF BEANSTALK'S LESSON BOOK PREP A.

12545

COOL GROOVES

Steadily

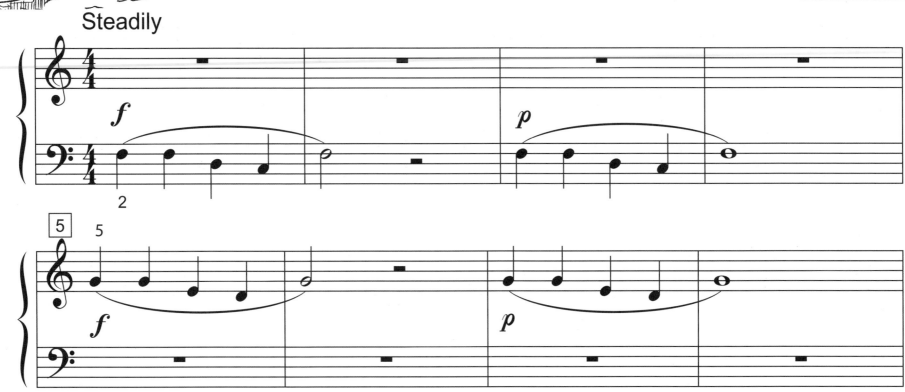

Student plays one octave higher than written.

Steadily

Teacher Duet Part

CORRESPONDS WITH PAGES 3 THROUGH 11 OF BEANSTALK'S LESSON BOOK PREP B.

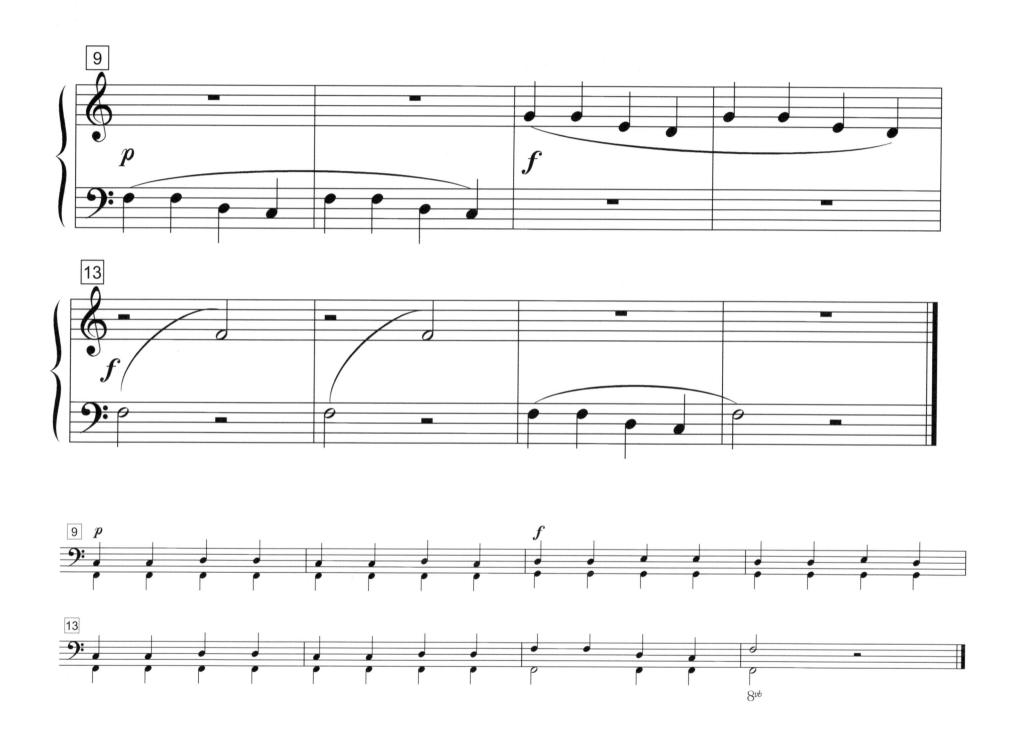

INDIAN VILLAGE

ENCORE!

6. Memorized.

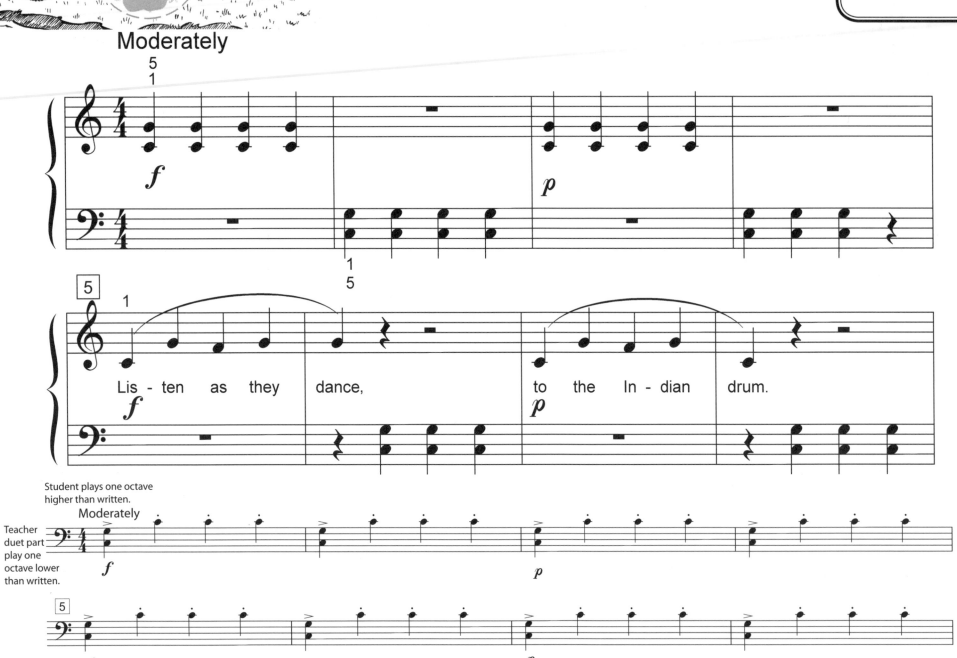

CORRESPONDS WITH PAGES 12 THROUGH 17 OF BEANSTALK'S LESSON BOOK PREP B.

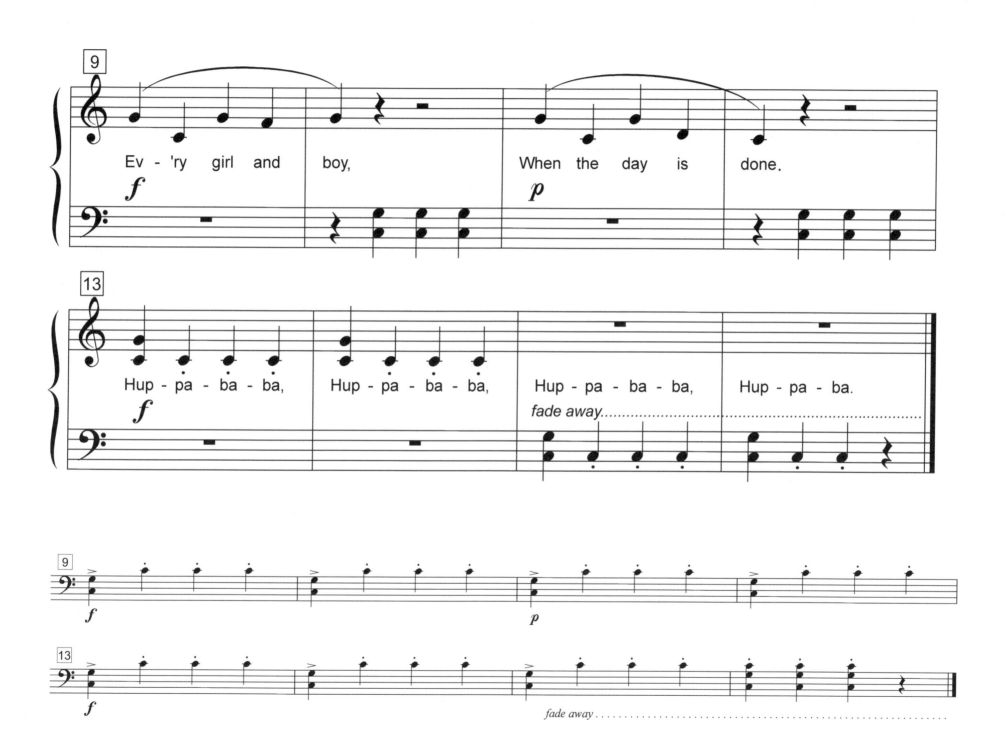

PERFORMANCE NOTES

To play an octave higher than written means to play eight notes higher. For example, an octave higher than E is the next E above.

USING THE PEDAL

Most pianos have **THREE** pedals. For this piece we will be using the pedal on the right which is called the **DAMPER PEDAL**.

Only use your right foot to play the damper pedal and **ALWAYS KEEP YOUR HEEL ON THE FLOOR!**

Simply push down the damper pedal at the start of this piece, and lift it at the end. You'll notice that as the sounds blur together they create a dream-like effect!

DAYDREAMS

Both hands play one octave higher than written. **Dreamily**

Let's pre - tend,   Let's pre - tend.   In our day - dreams let's pre - tend.

Student plays one octave higher than written.

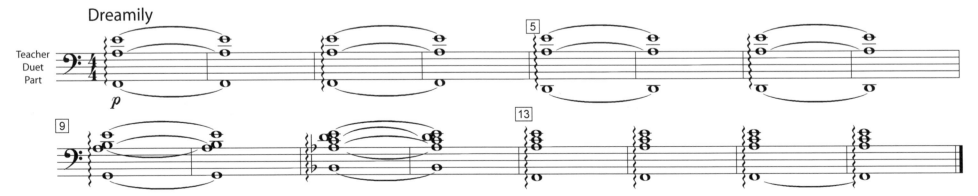

Dreamily

Teacher Duet Part

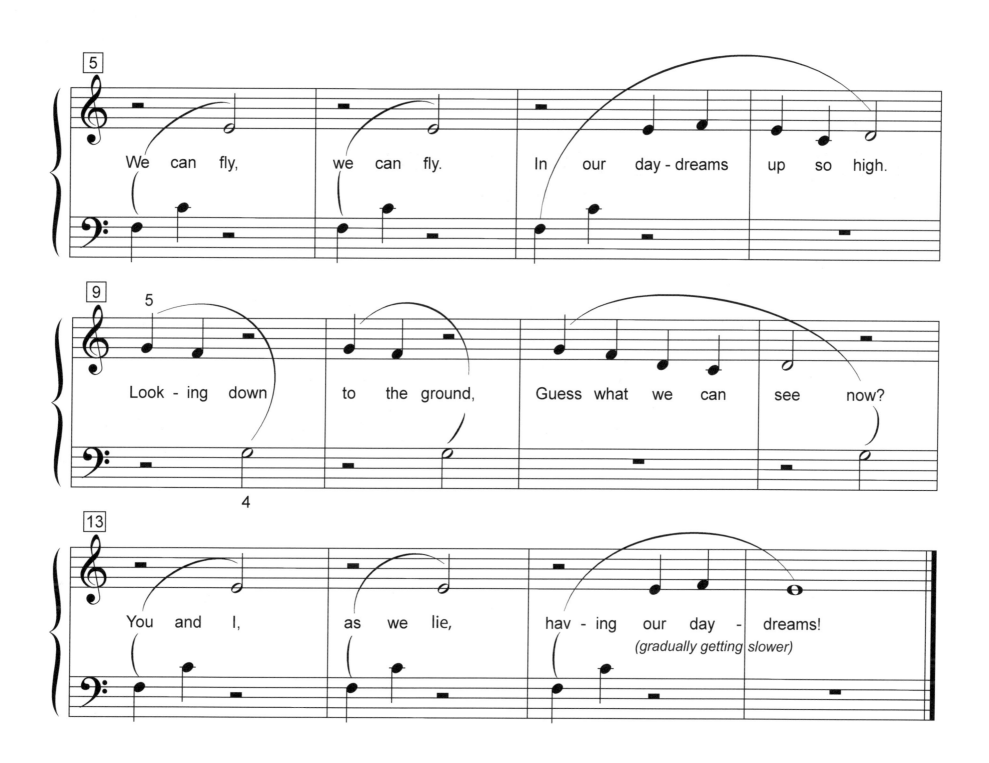

GHOST STORY

(for Marcel Tomkulak)

Mysteriously!

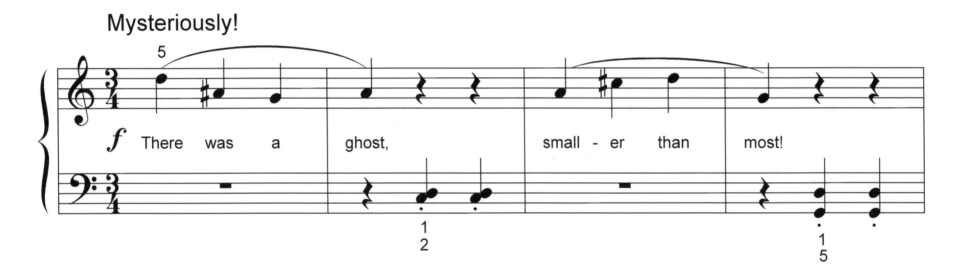

There was a ghost, small - er than most!

Student plays one octave higher than written.

Mysteriously!

Teacher duet part play one octave lower than written.

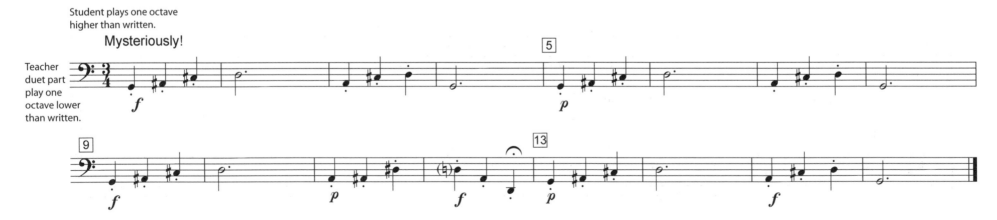

CORRESPONDS WITH PAGES 25 THROUGH 33 OF BEANSTALK'S LESSON BOOK PREP B.
12545

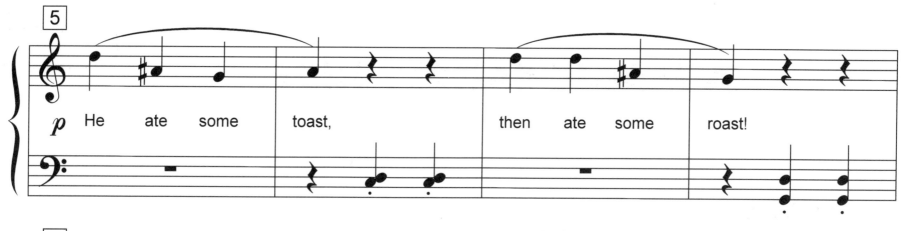

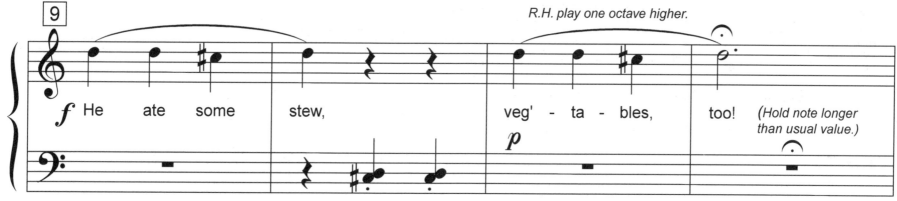

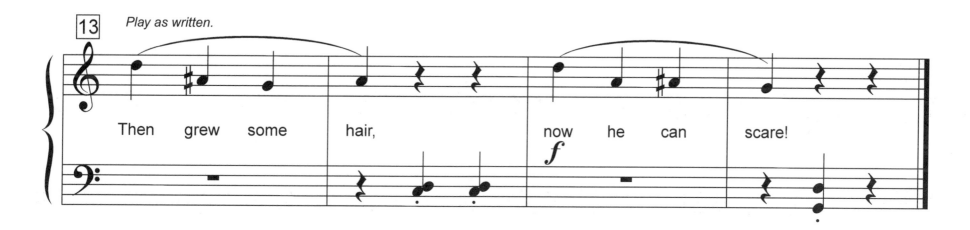

A MAGIC CARPET RIDE

Moderately

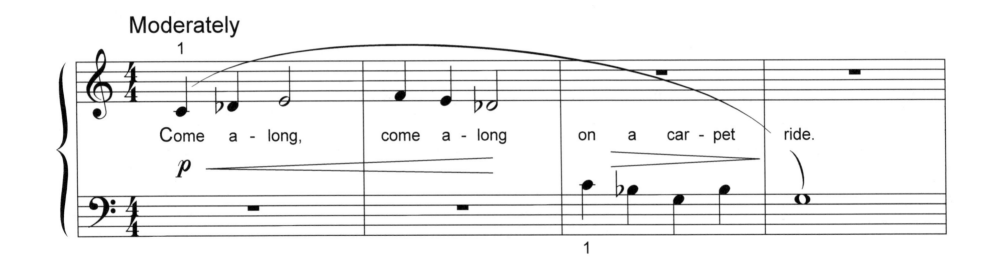

Come a - long, come a - long on a car - pet ride.

Student plays as written.

Moderately

Teacher duet part play one octave lower than written.

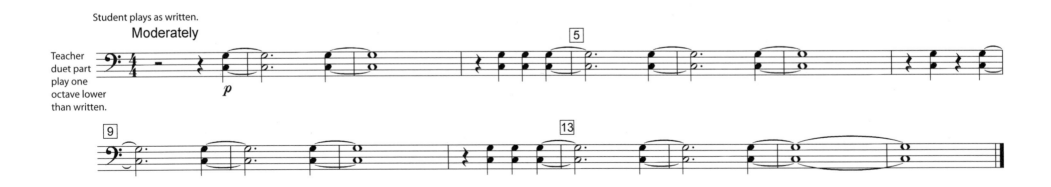

CORRESPONDS WITH PAGES 34 THROUGH 39 OF BEANSTALK'S LESSON BOOK PREP B.

Play one octave higher.   *Play two octaves higher.* _____

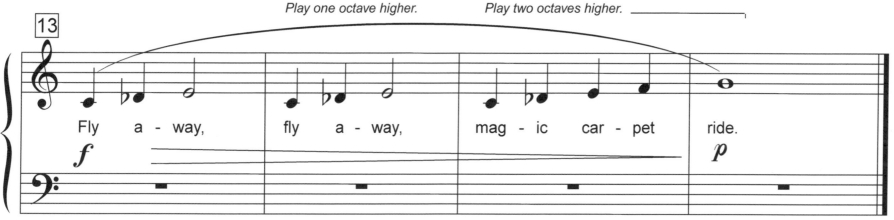

Hold down pedal to the end.

CRAZY CLOWNS!

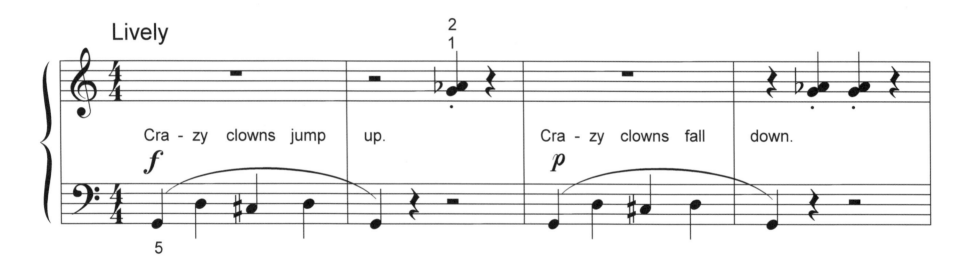

Lively

Cra - zy clowns jump up. Cra - zy clowns fall down.

Student plays one octave higher than written.

Lively

Teacher duet part play one octave lower than written.

gliss

rit.

CORRESPONDS WITH PAGES 40 THROUGH 45 OF BEANSTALK'S LESSON BOOK PREP B.

Certificate of Performance

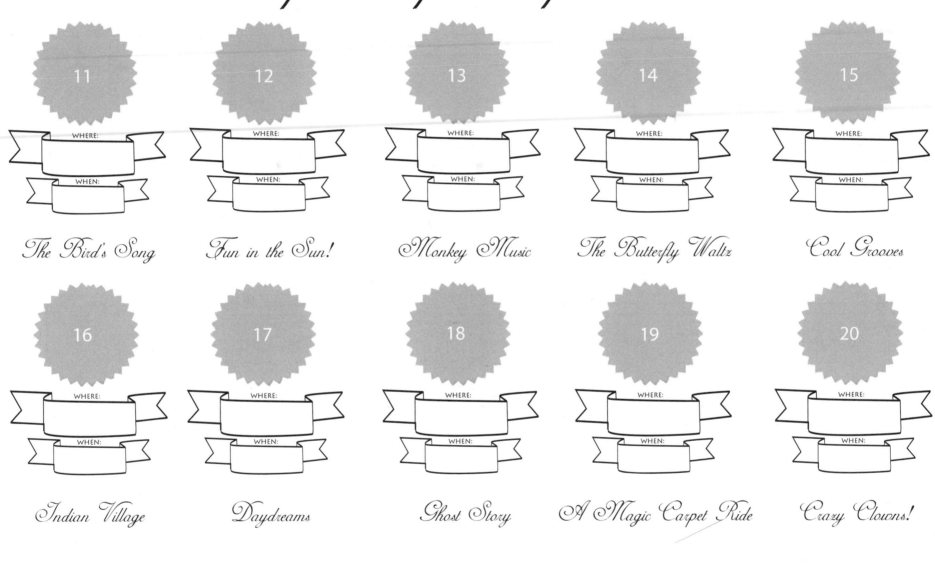

11 — WHERE: WHEN:
The Bird's Song

12 — WHERE: WHEN:
Fun in the Sun!

13 — WHERE: WHEN:
Monkey Music

14 — WHERE: WHEN:
The Butterfly Waltz

15 — WHERE: WHEN:
Cool Grooves

16 — WHERE: WHEN:
Indian Village

17 — WHERE: WHEN:
Daydreams

18 — WHERE: WHEN:
Ghost Story

19 — WHERE: WHEN:
A Magic Carpet Ride

20 — WHERE: WHEN:
Crazy Clowns!

_____

name of student

Successfully performed all pieces in Beanstalk's Performance Book Preparatory Level.
You are now promoted to Beanstalk's Performance Book Level One.

Date: _____   Teacher: _____